THE FACE

CARTOGRAPHY
OF THE VOID

CHRIS ABANI

THE FACE

CARTOGRAPHY OF THE VOID

RESTLESS BOOKS
BROOKLYN, NEW YORK

Cover design by Kristen Radtke
Set in Garibaldi by Tetragon, London

Library of Congress Cataloging-in-Publication
Data: Available upon request.

ISBN: 978-1-63206-0-433

Printed in the United States of America

Ellison, Stavans, and Hochstein LP
232 3rd Street, Suite A111
Brooklyn, NY 11215
www.restlessbooks.com
publisher@restlessbooks.com

THRESHOLD

BROTHER: You're writing an essay on your face?
ME: Yep. Book length.
BROTHER: [Pause.] So a short book, then?

CAVEAT

EVERYTHING IN THIS BOOK is true, even when the facts have been blunted by time and memory; even as I misremember, even as I misrepresent.

Everything in this book is a remembrance, so none of it may be true at all.

But it doesn't matter.

A SLOW VIOLENCE

THERE ARE NO easy ways to speak these words. No way to honor love and truth without something getting lost in translation. It is made even more complex when one party is dead, silent to this world. And how do you tell a story that is commonplace and felt by all without giving in to sentimentality? But the thing is that, in the end, we each must decide how comfortable we are with how much we hurt other people.

ORIENTATION

THIS ESSAY IS NOT just an exploration of my physical face; it is about the face we all identify with. It is about more than just what flesh covers my bone structure. It is about reflection, too. What we see or want to see in the mirror.

Biologically my face is a mix of two races, of two cultures, of two lineages. One white—English, perhaps a mix of Celt and Anglo-Saxons. My maternal grandmother's lineage was Strong, first held by a family in Somerset that predated the Norman Conquest. Strong of course referred to a person who displayed those characteristics in some way—physical, mental, even by way of dress, as in dressing for strength, which might have included armor in the past, or style in the present. In the Old High German it was Streng, which is related to String. A line, a connection, lineage. On my maternal grandfather's side, it is Hunt—from hunta, which is a hunter. They came from Shropshire and again predate the Norman Conquest. Strong Hunt, Hunt Strong.

Before the Engle (Angle) and the Saxon, early Germanic tribal amalgamations settled in Great Britain. In the Middle Ages, the areas of Somerset and Shropshire were occupied by Celts. The Cornovii occupied the area of Shropshire and the Dumnonii the area of Somerset.

The Celts were headhunters and hard to subdue (much like my Afikpo ancestors in Nigeria) and their swords, the falcata, were curved in the right way to hook a head on the backswing of a slash. The falcata was a specialized weapon and could not be used everyday. This was both its strength and weakness. The Saxons, however, defeated the Celts with the weapon they were named after, the seax, an unusually versatile sword. Fifteen hundred years ago, swords were expensive, and so the Saxon warrior farmers needed a knife that could double as a weapon—hence the seax. The fact that they were always armed this way meant that they could catch the Celts off guard and unarmed. In Afikpo, you receive the knife, which is both for farming and taking heads, as part of your initiation into manhood. Ceremonially you wear the mask mma ji, or yam knife. These are the people I come from. A long line of noble people, a long line of mongrels. That is one story of my lineage. Another is that my maternal grandfather got his name from Henry John Hunter, a trader who made his fortune in the romantic East and returned to buy the Beech Hill Estate in Berkshire. Was he a relative, or was he the child of an indentured worker? Whatever the case, my maternal grandparents are from the

Windsor basin of Berkshire, and they were first cousins.

But for all that, this essay is not about them. But about my father and the lineage I know for sure. The Egu and Ehugbo.

PHOTOGRAPHS

IN A VARIETY of faded black-and-white prints, my ancestors, at least those who lived to see the invention of the camera, stare back at me. There are more photos of the white side of my family. Grandparents and great-grandparents—the former already leaning into the informality of the 1920s in their dress and stances, the latter buttoned up in heavy black Victorian clothes, their lips unsmiling, set into disapproving lines.

The indexical quality of photographs means that, in their own way, they become a kind of shadow archive of your life, your lineage. As with all archives, the personal and the public can overlap, forming a system of classification. Classifications that become a system of determining and even legitimizing impressions, ideas, and even belief systems, forging them into truths.

In this one photograph my father smiles at me. He is in his early 20s, flanked by two heavyset Irish priests. I crop the priests out and enlarge his face. If I print a transparency of a photo of my own face in my 20s and lay it over his, it is possible we would look nothing alike. It is possible we would look exactly alike.

CALL

OTHER BROTHER: Hey, G. says you're asking for face jokes.

ME: Not really.

OTHER BROTHER: I've got a good one. You'll thank me later.

ME: Fine.

OTHER BROTHER: Kid says, Mommy, all the kids at school say I'm a werewolf! Is it true? Mom says, of course not. Now shut up and comb your face. What do you think?

ME: Fuck Google.

FACE VALUE

WHEN I TELL PEOPLE that my mother was a white Englishwoman and my father Igbo, they look at me skeptically. It's a pause that really means, "Are you sure? You're so dark." It's a pause that I've heard only in the West. In Nigeria most people know upon meeting me that I'm not entirely African. Nigeria has a long history of foreigners coming through—the Portuguese in the fourteenth century, North Africans as far back as the twelfth century, Tuaregs and Fulani to name just a few. In fact, in the late '80s and early '90s the civil war in Chad caused the very light-skinned Chadians to pour into Nigeria as refugees. It was a disturbing sight to see hundreds, sometimes thousands, of homeless Arab-looking people begging for food in the streets and markets. The public outcry was so severe that the military government began a program of forced repatriation. Army trucks rolled into markets and soldiers would round up these refugees, separating families without a second thought—after all, they all looked alike—and drive them back to the border. I once found myself being pushed into one such truck, but my fluency in several Nigerian languages saved me. I was often confused for being Lebanese, Indian, Arab, or Fulani. But not in England or America. In these places I am firmly black, of unknown origin.

But people have learned to be polite here, so no one says anything that might offend. They nod and make murmuring noises instead; except the LAPD, whose officers took great offense at my still very English accent when I arrived in LA. They asked me why I was faking it. I never quite figured out why, but whatever the reason, they were always very offended when I was pulled over.

It is interesting that I would be suspected of lying about my mixed-raced heritage. As though I was seeking some privilege, some "betterment" of my black lot, because, well, everyone knows some white in you is better than none, right? Wrong.

When we were kids in London, my mother was often congratulated for adopting us. It still amazes me that she never grew tired of correcting people, and not always kindly. In the '90s I was standing next to my mother at an ATM in London and we were chatting as she withdrew money. A policeman wandered over and casually asked my mother if she was okay and if I was trying to rob her. And one of my agents, on meeting my mother at an awards ceremony in LA, exclaimed, "Oh my God, she's as white as day."

Frantz Fanon has written better than I ever will about this matter: the idea of whiteness, and a visible whiteness, being preferred; the idea that secretly all white people believe that everyone really wants to look like them, to be them.

Face value, an interesting term, has many origins. It refers to the value of money based on the sum printed on its face. There was no need to bite the coin to see if it was gold or weigh it to see if it was an alloy. There was nothing hidden. But what claims to uncover, to reveal, can often obfuscate. If there is face value, a fiat of measure, then the opposite is implied—apparent value; as in, don't accept promises or claims of face value.

Growing up in Nigeria, my brother Greg was very light-skinned, and of all of us he had the longest, straightest hair. "Mbunu Jesus," my aunt would say, which loosely translates to "He's just like Jesus." The nickname stuck for a long time. When I was out and about with Greg we must have made quite a picture—Greg skinny with long hair and me plump and with kinky hair.

In the usual way of people in Afikpo they would ask, "Who claims you?" A way of ascertaining your lineage, determining whether they needed to know more. Only when you had been located in a lineage of repute would the follow-up be "What is your name?" In our case, the next question would be "You are brothers?" Yes. "Same mother, same father?" Yes. Then with a mix of pity and mockery they would ask me, "So, what happened to you?"

Face value.

In taxicabs in Nigeria, or buses, people would talk about me, referring to me as korawayo, a nickname for foreigners (particularly Lebanese) who exploited and cheated Nigerians. I would sit silently, listening to the badmouthing until I would casually ask in Igbo (fluently), Yoruba (less fluently), or Hausa (even less fluently) what the time was or some such question. The effect was hilarious, the embarrassment and apologies profuse.

When I lived in East Los Angeles, a predominately Chicano/Latino neighborhood, I was assumed to be Dominican or Panamanian. In Miami, where I go regularly for religious reasons, I am confused for a Cuban. In New Zealand I was assumed to be Maori. In Australia, Aborigine. In Egypt, Nubian. In Qatar, Pakistani. In South Africa, Zulu or some other group, depending on who was talking. Other times, because of my accent, which is a mix of Nigerian, British, and now American inflections, I am assumed to be from "one of the islands." No one accepts my Nigerianness, not without argument. In fact, the two things I have been rarely taken for—Nigerian and white—are the very things that form my DNA.

Face value.

Agemo, the Yoruba say. Chameleon.

Most of the confusion about who I am is a product of how my face is read. Thus it is perceived to be where it is thought to belong. And how it is supposed to look.

As my father used to say in the heavy Igbo accent he would adopt when particularly disgusted by some new facet of my rebellion, "You are just a disappointment."

Even my grandfather, who cast kola nuts when I was born and who nicknamed me Erusi (spirit), would shake his head and say, "You don't belong here or in the land of the spirits. You are a bat, neither bird nor mammal." I loved that. That meant I could be anything.

Even Batman.

THE PERFORMANCE

THE FACE IN AFIKPO is a stage, a state of flux, of becoming. The face is a performance, an enactment by the animating consciousness behind it. When used with intent, it is the performance of awareness behind it. So, in this way, the face is both the portal and that which is transported.

My elders say it like this:

Ihu dike bu ihe eji ama nwoke.
(The face of the warrior is how we measure a man.)
Essence: character.

Ihu ezenze bu ihe eji ama uwa.
(The face of an elder is how we learn/
understand the world.)
Essence: experience.

Ihu juujuu bu ihe eji ama dimkpa.
(The face of calmness is how we measure a
person's importance/power.)
Essence: serenity.

Ihu mma bu ihe eji ama dibia.
(The face of spirit reveals the diviner.)
Essence: wisdom.

The face and its value lay in its ability to reference
and perform, which is to manifest the true nature
or character behind it.

Akara ihu bu obi madu.
(The lines on the face reveal a person's heart.)
Essence: the wise augur.

Lines on the outer face lead to what lies not just inside us, but also through a dream-time to our ancestral lineage, to our culture, to the very soul of our land and our people. These lines and the other physical oddities of the face mark the terrain of self and culture, of a community or even communities, at once obvious and yet simultaneously occluded.

ON BEAUTY

IN WESTERN THOUGHT, composition creates beauty. Perspective. Symmetry. The Golden Ratio. An impossible one-sided ideal. In West African thought, composure creates beauty. Balance. Equanimity. Serenity. The essential nature of a thing. Its ase.

In Yoruba Iwalewa is beauty, and it means the beauty of truth or even the beauty of existence. The word Iwa is best translated to mean existence, an eternal state, being outside of time. Reality is held in Igba Iwa, the calabash of existence. Iwa is connected to an old idea that holds that immortality is the perfect existence, or better, a timelessness.

It suggests that all temporality has ramification in an eternal cycle of existence—at an individual level, at a communal and lineage level, at a cultural level, and, in many ways, at a planetary level. Everyone's Iwa is always part of the Igba Iwa, and the perfect balance between all Iwas depends on the singular balance of each.

Ewa, in Yoruba, is a word that means beauty. But beauty is a complex concept in West Africa. It doesn't refer only to the visage of things. In Igbo, beauty, nma, is also the word for good, meaning that what is beautiful is good as well. But with a slight inflection it is also the word for knife or even machete—a warning. On one hand, good is a behavioral matrix, and on the other, it is an appreciative matrix, but in both cases it is a communal process. Beauty is not a concept that works in isolation. One cannot be good or beautiful without the participation of others. But there are concepts of beauty in Igbo that are valued even more:

Asa Mpete; a beauty in movement, in being, in face, completeness.

Nganga; grace, poise, elegance.

Oma; self-awareness, collectedness, balance.

Ewa doesn't refer to composition in the Western sense. It refers to an essential conformity to an inner trait. Hence driftwood is beautiful because it conforms to its inner trait; it bends with its ase, which is always there but only revealed to us over time. So beauty is a state of existence. Iwalewa is an existence in and as beauty. Since Iwa refers to the eternal constant of a person or thing or even sometimes a place, to create beauty (or even to perceive it) is to capture (or see) the essential nature of that thing. Beauty in West African thought lies in recognizing and respecting the uniqueness of all things and all people. To do this, in Yoruba it is said that one must cultivate patience, suuru. Patience is the shape respect takes, and this is a necessary practice, because it is important for West Africans that we understand the essential beauty of whatever confronts us before revealing ourselves or acting. So this respect, which might be better thought of as a thoughtful restraint, is twofold—self-respect and the respect of others—and is itself a form of Iwalewa. So we comprehend the essential beauty of everyone and everything around us, and we in turn become beautiful; as the Igbo say, ugwu bu nkwanye nkwanye—respect is reciprocal. For the Igbo, external beauty matches eternal beauty such that the eagle, a common ideal of beauty, is beautiful as much for the way light shimmers through the water in its feathers in flight as it is for the totality of the eagle. To see beauty is to be beauty, therefore beauty is about coming into an understanding of one's own Iwa, or essential nature, the practice of which involves Ifarabale (calmness), Imoju-imora (perception and sensitivity), Tito (gentleness), Oju inu (insight), and Oju ona (originality). To be an artist in Yoruba culture is to possess a cool and patient character (Iwa tutu, ati suruu).

Look at the faces of Nok terracotta sculpture and see the composure of being-ness—serenity, calmness, and equanimity. Even warriors on horseback gaze into infinity with a patient calmness.

A cursory glance at the Ife and Benin bronze sculptures reveal this attitude toward beauty. In all Yoruba sculpture, the head is always out of proportion to the body, not from any lack of artistic ability, but to emphasize philosophical and spiritual concepts of the head. Ori Ode is the house of the eternal spirit and mind, Ori Inu, and thus the arbiter of human destiny. Iwa in Yoruba and Uwa/Owa in Igbo are key to the understanding of beauty and the self.

In this way, even in these West African cultures, beauty is still tied to the face (even when thought of as a portal) and thus to power. It is important to wear the right face. To face the world with the right relationship to Iwa, the right power, to reveal nothing, to keep a poker face, not to lose face. And in the end it all cycles back. The older Western cultures probably shared the same understanding of beauty and the face, but much of what we now think of as Western thought is a product of the paranoia of the Renaissance and the so-called Enlightenment and the more recent neuroses generated during the Industrial Revolution.

The gulf in perception/worldview or, should I say, in the conceptual premises between Africa and the West, can be understood by considering the process of naming, of how being-ness comes about. Consider the naming of a child. In the West names are nominal, but in West Africa they are phenomenal. Names in West Africa are arrived at via consultation (divinatory, oracular, or by consultation within family), and the name chosen reflects the essential character, Iwa or Uwa/Owa, of the new person. It also becomes a performative talisman to constantly manifest that state.

For instance in Igbo, to be named Ihuoma ("good face" or "beautiful face") refers not just to the physical features; it also means that goodness and beauty lie ahead for this person if they cultivate the right "face."

THIS IS TRUE

1. My dead father and I look alike. I wear his face.
2. My father tried his whole life to be a good man.
3. My father was generous to the world and to strangers.
4. My father was stingy at home, with money and his emotions.
5. My father made strangers laugh.
6. My father and I have never laughed together.
7. My father cheated on my mother constantly.
8. My father grew up poor. His father was a houseboy for Catholic priests.

9. My father wore his father's face.

10. My father barely spoke to his father.

11. My grandfather tried to keep my father from taking the scholarship the Church offered him.

12. At twenty-three he had never been more than a hundred miles from my town.

13. At twenty-three, my father left for the University of Cork, Ireland and later Oxford.

14. My father was the first university graduate from my town.

15. My father came back in 1956 with a white woman.

16. My father married that white woman in 1957 in my small town.

17. My father beat my mother. Often. I still carry the guilt of my helplessness.

18. My father, outside of monogamy, was the most honest man I have ever known.

19. My father made me the man I am today.

20. My father loved me even though violence was his preferred mode of affection.
21. My father was raised to be a warrior.
22. My father was a school principal.
23. My father was a member of parliament in the first republic.
24. My father was a state superintendent of schools.
25. My father was the federal commissioner for public complaints.
26. My father was a customary court chairman.
27. My father was not required to be a warrior in any of these roles.
28. My father brought the war home to us every night and fought his demons.
29. My father's demons were his family, apparently.
30. My father tried to self-medicate, but the alcohol only made it worse.
31. My father educated me.

32. My father kept me on the straight and narrow.

33. My father taught me that, even when it hurts you and others, loyalty is absolute.

34. My father tried to beat the creative and artistic leanings out of us.

35. My father wanted us to have sensible jobs.

36. My father played jazz piano at Oxford.

37. My father is easier to love as a spirit, a ghost, than as a man.

38. My father's face stares back at me from the mirror.

39. My father has been forgiven.

THIS IS NOT A SITCOM

TO SAY IT IS important in Afikpo for a man to have children, male children in particular, is to understate things. It is in fact essential. A man's progress in Afikpo culture, the various titles he can take and the honor they bestow, is only possible through sons. Sons are so important that if a rich man doesn't have a son he will "borrow" one, a surrogate, pay for his initiation into manhood, and thus advance his own status as a man who has birthed a warrior. Since girls in the old days were often married off early, the idea of lineage is only possible with sons. A woman who has sons is important; her marriage may fail, she may be a bad cook, but with sons she has status amongst women and respect from men. And so my mother, a foreigner, a white woman, became a favored adopted daughter in my father's lineage when she gave him four sons in succession.

When a son is born, it sets off a series of rituals towards manhood. Events which not only advance the status of the son but also bring prestige to his father.

Traditionally children are born with the mother kneeling or squatting low, and the newborn touches the ground on its way out of the birth canal, cementing the connection between the birth mother and the All Mother, the earth. Childbirth is an exclusive arena for women in Afikpo. Not even male herbalists or priests attend a birth unless it is absolutely essential. It is the exclusive work of women, not because it is demeaning; on the contrary, it is because it is elevating. The ability to give birth, in Afikpo cosmology, elevates women to the level of the creator. It is a moment of primordial connection with the holiest mystery, and men are considered unable and unworthy to stand in the full presence of God. A secret ritual unknown to anyone but the mothers is performed at birth, and the umbilical and placenta are buried in the family compound to place the child under the protection of the earth and all the ancestral lineage of that child.

Only when the women send up the call "Okoko-riko!"—the call of the rooster—are men allowed to visit. The rituals of manhood begin almost immediately, but these would take a whole book to explain. Suffice it to say that I was born in a hospital, after my mother had been in labor for nearly seventy-two hours. She lost so much blood that she nearly died. And by the time my umbilical and placenta had been taken back to the homestead and buried, my father was already unhappy with me. I was a son who had nearly killed his mother.

And to make matters worse, I was not even the son of honor (the firstborn) or the son of war (the second son) or the son of the farm (the third son), but the fourth son, with a destiny of either ordinariness or the power to become the diviner, which made me both useless and terrifying at the same time. To be the unremarkable fourth son and potential mother-killer was enough to make me useless in my father's eyes.

That I was born just weeks before the civil war arrived in our town cemented his disregard. "You should not have survived the flight from the war," he told me when I was a teenager. "You should have died then." It at least would have given him a son who had died an honorable death. Later, as I grew up, I sensed that the four-year gap between my immediate elder brother and me had not been caused by careful planning but by a possible abortion after a pregnancy from an affair. So even though I was the spitting image of my father, I might have also looked like the man who cuckolded him. This was the relationship I believed I had with my father—the son whose every choice would disappoint. One could even argue that I excelled at this disappointment and that I continue to disappoint because I always choose my own path. A path marked for me by my Owa, not by expectation.

I had no evidence for believing that my father didn't truly love me, no real way to prove a lack of paternal affection. Violence alone was not proof. In a culture where kids are punished with beatings, it is not seen as abuse or lack of love. Perhaps the position my father's generation found themselves in, not in line with the old ways and teetering on the edge of the new, was the culprit. In traditional Igbo culture, beatings were followed with reaffirmations of love; it was not unlike the joke here in the United States about parents giving us the belt and the line "This is going to hurt me more than you." There was never the balm of soothing words for me post-beating. There was only the affirmation that this had been deserved and was a result of my own lack. Maybe. Maybe it also lay in something unique to me, the betrayal of my own expectations of how I wanted to be loved, a desire that was unfair to put on someone.

Growing up middle-class in Nigeria at the time that I did created conflicting expectations. My father's generation was the first to transition en masse from a more rural, traditional culture to the middle-class elite realities of post-independence Nigeria. He struggled to balance out the warrior training he had grown up with against the new possibilities and demands of being his town's first graduate, and from Oxford no less. My generation struggled to reconcile the often conflicting, schizophrenic expectations of our parents' old-world ideals and punishments with the equally schizophrenic Western ideals of parenting we saw on television. These came to a head with the Cosby Show.

I said to my father, "Dr. Huxtable tells his son, 'Theo, I love you,' and all you do is yell at me and tell me how I fail. How I embarrass you. How I betray you." He was eating. He paused and looked up at me from the plate and said, "Shut your mouth before I rearrange your stupid face."

Again, the face. That face. Always.

TEXT MESSAGE

BROTHER: Why did the pig have ink all over its face?

ME: I'll regret this, but why?

BROTHER: Cause it came out of the pen.

ME: I can't use any of these.

BROTHER: Fine. But here's another. Did you hear about the witch who went to audition for TV and was told she had the perfect face for radio?

ME: Look...

BROTHER: One last one. You have the face of a saint.

ME: Which one?

BROTHER: St. Bernard. Hahahaha.

ME: Googling again?

BROTHER: How can you tell?

TO CHEW PEPPER

THIS IS HOW BOYS are presented to the world at birth. This is the name of the ceremony. To chew pepper is to be a man. To be able to withstand the rigors and complexities ahead, to be fortified against defeat, against life. To chew pepper is to have dominion over the earth. This ceremony is the greatest gift a father can give his son. It is usually reserved for the first son, but those fathers who can afford it, those who want to, those who secretly care about their other sons, perform the ceremony for every male child.

Even though we follow a double-descent paradigm in Afikpo, the pepper-chewing ceremony is only for the patrilineal line. The men gather in a circle in the family courtyard and the oldest male, who is also the priest of the family shrine, sits on a stool in the center with the child on his lap. Then the child's father brings the following items, and the old man presents them to the child, intoning:

"Here is mma ji (yam knife/warrior knife). May whatever you grow flourish. May your enemies fall to you."

"Here is opia (a bush-clearing knife/head-hunting knife). If you go out to the field, may your right hand be up, may you be the first man to cut, may the bush and your enemies fall at your feet."

"Here is mpana (farm knife/sword). The work of growth is hard, that of killing fast. May you grow more than you kill."

"Here is arua (a thin, three-foot-long spear). Hold it true, skewer your gain, be it meat or man."

"Here is agbo (thick fiber belt for climbing trees). May you climb to any height and not fall."

Then the old man takes the hot peppers the father passes to him, chews them with dried fish and yam, and places them on the child's lips. The burn wakes the child up, as it does the gods, fortifying him, making him able to face any difficulty in the world.

Then everyone prays for the child, for his long life, for his success, for his uprightness, for his good character, for him to be serene of face.

Then the old man takes water (representing palm wine) in a calabash and pours it on the slanting roof of a nearby house. He does it four times, each time touching the calabash to the child's feet and then to the ground. The upward thrust of the calabash is to make the boy fearless and unafraid, the water running down the roof is rain and the fecundity of life, and the ground is the mother that roots him always. And in this way the boy is introduced to the world, to both the sky and the earth, the father and mother, the very heart of existence.

I have eaten peppers all my life.

I must be a woman. I must be a mother.

I must be a man. I must be my father.

This is your father's face.

Wear it.

LAVENDER

FOR YEARS THERE WAS a scar under my bottom lip, one I wore with pride. When I was maybe four I fell running in a park in Burnham and drove my two top teeth through my bottom lip. There was blood everywhere. And as I trembled in shock, a kind and suave Englishman with a cane picked me up and pressed his pocket square that smelled of lavender to my wound. "Who's a brave chap?" he asked. "Brave chaps don't cry, all right old boy?" I nodded, pressing the square of fabric into my chin as my mother came rushing up. As she grew frantic, the man put his hand on her shoulder and said, "It's all right, he's a real gentleman. Gentlemen are always all right." And he was gone. Every time I try to summon his face all I see are pocket squares, a gold signet ring, and a cane, and there is also the lingering smell of lavender.

I didn't know this, but for years this was the shape of my yearning for a different father. I was eighteen months old when we fled Biafra, and I had no memory of my father. Still, I must have been searching for him. And I found him in that scar and that smell.

There are other scars on my body, caused by or shared with my real father. I'm proud of those too. There is a six-inch scar that runs down my left shin, a curved centipede of a thing. Twenty-six stitches when I was just six. I had slipped and fallen on the jagged point of a broken bottle. The glass cut to the bone. As he rushed me to the hospital, my father was torn between his fear that I might bleed out and his exhortations to keep my leg off the cloth seat of his pristine Peugeot 301.

And the scars on the back of his right hand that he told me were caused by shrapnel from a grenade he caught to save a small child. My mother later told me he got them in a drunken fight with his brother, Emmanuel, who cut him with the sharp end of a broken beer bottle. These were the same scars I sank my teeth into, drawing blood, when he slapped me for the first time. I was five. That bite earned me a left hook to the side of the head, but it was worth it to know I had left a mark on him. The next day I lost three milk teeth. It was an endless bargain of violence.

And the scars on his back cut deep from the initiation whips and the manhood rite of Iti Osiosi (literally "to beat sticks"), a rite in which all young men, myself included, participated. We would strip to the waist and gather in the communal playground. Submit your back to be whipped, and if you didn't cry out or shed a tear, you won and your opponent had to present his back to you. The first to cry was out. To prove how brave we were we jockeyed for the right to present our backs first. In my father's day the scars were as severe as the whipping. But we were gentler with each other, and so the scars were so slight that they quickly faded to psychic imprints. But they never leave you—the cut of the chili-and urine-soaked whips that ripped flesh, the snarl of pleasure on your opponent's face, and the tears blinked back for your manhood. That was the journey for me: give and take, whip and be whipped, skin for blood, blood for skin.

Scars and the lingering smell of Old Spice. Our lives are a series of losses and gains.

THE TERRAIN

IT IS DIM in the museum in Auckland, New Zealand. Even dark, and moody. Light filters into this room in a hush, as if afraid to disturb something that lurks inside the shadows of the replica wharenui sitting in the middle of the room.

A wharenui (big house) or whare whakairo (carved house) is the focal point of a Maori marae, the communal space marked off for ritual and sacred ceremonies. Inside and outside of the wharenui are stylized carved images of the iwi, the tribe's ancestors. But the wharenui is itself an ancestor too, perhaps the primordial founder of the tribe. I confess my knowledge here is limited, but if the wharenui is an ancestor, the koruru, or gable, at the front represents the head; the maihi, the diagonal baseboards, signify arms; the tahuhu, or the ridge beam, is the backbone; the heke, or rafters, signify ribs; and the central column inside, the poutokomanawa, is the heart.

I stand there and I don't just breathe in the wood smell and the acridity of new wood polish; I am also reminded in this moment that all old cultures are more alike than not.

Here I stand before the Obuogo, the men's sacred house at the center of the Ogo, in my hamlet of Amaha. It is the same principle, the same idea. Just as the wharenui is for the Maori, the Obuogo (the spiritual heart of the Ogo) is the center of the space of mystery and ancestral worship (Ogo), and the insides are lined with carved and sculpted ancestors. The two main differences are that Obuogos are made of mud walls built around wood frames with a raffia roof, and that the heart of the Obuogo is not a pillar but a room with an even smaller room inside it. The outer room houses the ancestral masks for the masquerades and other such paraphernalia and even, in some cases, the kamalu pots of the men, our ancestral lineage pots. The smaller room houses the secrets of Egbele and Okemma, the spirits that only the priests can know.

In the museum in Auckland, I reach out to the ancestral archetype closest to me. I am reminded of the role of this performative awe, which is to stress our links to both the living and the dead and to remind us that our identity is as much about the dead as it is about the living. In that mote-filled room I touch the ancestor's carved wooden face. If the docent sees me, he makes no attempt to stop me. On this trip I have been frequently confused for a Maori, even by Maoris, and it has led to some tense moments.

The wood is surprisingly soft. And oily from the polish I smelled earlier. In Amaha, the faces are covered in oily soot from fires and palm oil and rituals I cannot reveal here.

My finger travels the longest carved line on the face, the thickest welt, up that face. From the base of the jaw all the way up the cheek, stopping just short of the abalone shell eye. These lines cut into the wood are meant to mimic the ancient facial tattoos that marked these ancestors as men, as warriors, as worthy of carrying their lineage back into the place of death and yet forward into the place of tomorrow.

In that thought I was no longer in this museum in Auckland standing before a facsimile of the past but back in the small fishing and farming town of Afikpo and even smaller, back in the hamlet of Amaha, to be exact.

As the sun came through a cloud and lit up a face with carved teeth bared, lips curled back, tongue hanging out as though caught in a haka, the wooden lines became the scarification lines in the faces of my people, of a select few elders, ndegburuchi, those that cut ichi.

Practiced more prevalently among the northern Igbo of Nri descent, Igbuichi—literally "to cut ichi"—is an old practice that has mostly died out. Legend has it that it came to Afikpo with the Igala warriors who settled in Amachi (the hamlet of God) around the eighteenth century.

Igbo is a tonal language; the tonality of words define meaning, but they also allow punning, which is one of the linguistic ways the Ehugbo have of trying to account for the worldview of simultaneity that marks it—no pun intended here.

On the one hand, Ichi can mean to lead. Or to collect. To gather. Or it can mean to be in flow or accordance with your indwelling spirit, the spark of the creator we call Chi. The word, even when its tonality marks it one way, can and does also refer to all the above meanings. As we say in Afikpo: asusu bu uwa, language is the world.

Ichi were marks of status and rank, the mark of Igbo aristocracy, of the apex of both temporal and spiritual power. They were an immediate visual marker of extreme courage and endurance. Not all endured this form of extreme scarification, and succumbed to the effects of sepsis—sometimes losing an eye or both, sometimes a nose, sometimes their lives.

No one wearing Ichi was allowed to do any menial tasks, and they were never challenged or molested in any way. Even when the British colonized the country and met resistance led by those who bore Ichi, they never placed them in handcuffs when they arrested them but treated them as nobles.

Ichi was linked very much to the sun, and the marks were a way to wear the sun on your face. In Igbo the sun is called Anyaanwu, which means the eye or aura of the sun. The sun, anwu, was an entity that no one could behold with mortal eyes, and was considered the material expression of God's creative aspect, or the spiritualized notion of matter. The sun symbolized the highest form of light and purity and power, both spiritual and physical, such that it was a very high honor to wear it on your face. This is at one level what the scarification rite of Ichi meant.

The artist would cut the first line from the center of the forehead down to the chin. This was known as oyi agbara, the caul of the holy spirit. The second line was cut horizontally across the face, right to left, east to west, and was called ije enu—life's journey, the journey of the sun across the sky, the journey from life to death, and, as with the rising of the sun the next day, the resurrection and also reincarnation. In fact, in Afikpo the traditional morning greeting is Nnaa, to which the response is nnahicha. These are elisions of a larger saying: Nnaa is from the question "inahri onwu?" or "Did you escape death" (as sleep was seen as a small death), and the response, nnai-cha, is from "anahichari'm," "I escaped well." It is believed that to make the journey in full consciousness from birth to earth and to come back (either from sleep, trance, or meditation) with knowledge of the other side made one a great person. It is important to note that while most of those who wore ichi were men (as it required being a warrior too), women who were warriors (dike nwanyi) also could wear ichi. To wear ichi marked you as one who had lived a full life regardless of age, and one who by symbolic death and resurrection had become a living ancestor, one who it was believed could reincarnate parts of themselves while still alive.

The two first marks met at the bridge of the nose, oke igwe or the bridge of heaven; the cross, the place of balance. This pattern was then repeated sixteen times, sixteen being a number for creation, which created eight crosses, uwa'm uwa'm asaa, "my world my seven worlds," seven being how many incarnations it took for one complete human cycle (the eighth being the one being lived). The resulting pattern looked, in many ways, like the spread of an eagle's feathers, with the other figures being variations.

But besides marking a person into nobility, which was based not only on land and wealth and martial accomplishment, as is so often the case, ichi signified character and spiritual disposition. It served to a) obliterate the small human ego or facial identity and allow the spirit behind to shine through all the time, and b) form a mask (not unlike the beaded crowns of the Yoruba Obas) to protect the rest of the community from gazing into the pure power of the living ancestral spirit, much like the sun's rays form an aura to protect us from the true sun.

To cut ichi is to be reborn in light, in the path of true visions, to be held to a higher morality because it was impossible to hide the face, to disguise oneself and commit sins and crimes.

Onyegbuluchi refers to one who has cut ichi. It can also mean one who has killed (overcome or mastered) their spirit (chi) or destiny (chi). Like I said, to be Igbo is to live in convergence and simultaneity. To wear ichi was to wear your responsibility on your face. To wear your status as an elder, to always live up to the ideals of the community. Talk about stress lines!

Ironically, I am writing this in a new spring in Chicago, where the sun barely comes out. I stand sunning by the glass doors to the garden as often as I can. To sun the face. To wear the sun on the face. My grandfather was right: ejigi enya amaka ahu ime ogo, one cannot comprehend mystery with the outer eyes. Ihu umma bu ihe eji eje ali mma: the face of spirit is what we wear to the land of spirits.

THIS IS HOPE

1. That I can change.
2. That I can overcome my DNA.
3. That my nature will overcome nurture.
4. That I will leave a trail of love when I go.
5. That I will die trying to be a good man.
6. That all the hate dies with me.
7. That my face, and my father's face, and his father's face before him will blaze in an unending lineage of light and forgiveness.

PATER NOSTRA

OKPA IHU NNAYA—one who has his father's face. This was the affectionate term that my aunts on my father's side greeted me with. And yet I couldn't help thinking that under all that affection was an accusation. To have my father's face was to have taken it, stolen it perhaps, and to have refused to give it back. It also hinted at, I thought, a certain dishonesty on my part; rather than wear or reveal my face, I was hiding behind my father's. Other times I was called Ogbonnaya. Ogbo is a complex word; it means a male friend in the general sense but can also refer to a male friend who is specifically within one's own age grade, making them part of the same expression of time as you, bound by a communal obligation that lasts for life. Age grades in Afikpo and some other Igbo cultures are how things are governed. So to be ogbo nna, part of your father's age grade, that unique expression of life, could imply that you were in fact your father's clone. So closely did you resemble him that life had "stuttered" and created the same being twice. Of course the other part of this word, the friendship and ease, had to be present. You weren't just your father's clone, you were his favorite son, the closer one, the one who would be his confidant and, as much as was possible in Afikpo culture, his friend. It involves an active participation by the father. In my case, not so much. If others saw me as ogbo nnaya, my father saw me as his missed opportunities. As a doppelgänger that could and very well might take the road less traveled, which he had wanted but felt he couldn't choose because of family obligations.

He felt that he could very well watch me live the life that he had wanted, that he felt he deserved. With much compassion and understanding, I have come to realize, years after his death, that it was a thought he just couldn't stand. They say babies resemble their fathers at birth because it kept early humans from eating their own children. An evolutionary survival mechanism. My father didn't get that memo.

To wear the face of someone you can't help loving even as you can't help hating them, is to be caught in an infernal struggle for your own soul.

THE ARCHITECTURE OF LOSS

MY FACE IS THE MIRROR of a dead people—an extinct people. There is nothing left of my father's people, the Egu, other than a few ancestral masks that no one really understands anymore, a style of pottery that is still in use but accredited to another group, a few scattered and abandoned homesteads overgrown with weeds, and a few place names.

I touch my face in the mirror. Stubble. Acne scars. I am thinking of my father and his face. The sound of him shaving in the mornings, his cheeks, hardened over time, take the scrape of the razor with a wooden echo that I could hear down the hall. The deep black of his skin. A face like mine, all cheek and jowl. The way it would shut down into a sullen mask. Or twist into anger. Or the way his eyes would hood when he looked at you so that sometimes it was hard to tell if they were open. And the way sometimes that hooded look would carry menace and danger. These are all things my face does.

Every family has a hierarchy of pain, of loss, a narrative that each sibling holds—who got hurt most, who got left out, who never received enough love, or any of the love for that matter.

Every sibling will tell you that they had it worst growing up. These claims usually follow an age hierarchy, the eldest siblings claiming that parents were the strictest with them, the hardest on them.

In families with experiences of trauma, whether caused by external factors such as war or by internal factors such as a violent parent, the competitiveness is heightened. Which parent was more violent and to whom. It doesn't matter whether there are facts to be substantiated; emotional truth is all that counts in this game.

I had a defined mythology about my father and about how much harder he was on me, how much he hated me. I was clear about the ways in which he tried to destroy me. When I told my uncle that my father didn't love me, he looked at me confused. "But he has no choice," he said. "It is not a choice. He is your father." I have come to learn that there is truth to this. I have also come to learn that the other side of that truth is that your father can hate you for the ways in which he cannot help loving you. We are complex equations: fathers and sons.

And for many years I thought myself so different than he was, so much better. I prided myself on this difference. But everyone called me oyiri nnaya, the one who resembles his father. It chafed.

Then one day in my mother's small flat in Burnham, miles from him and years since I last saw him, I was making dinner with my brother

Greg and we were ribbing each other, and I laughed. My mother called out my father's name, Michael, and came stumbling into the kitchen with a dazed look on her face. "God, Christopher," she said. "You sound just like your father." I see it now. In my face, in my hands, in my gestures. I am just like my father, and twelve years after his death I can say it with pride, with an ease. I resemble my father. I am my father's son—and yet still there is a seed of doubt, and the texture of that doubt is the texture of my face, smooth but for the resistance of stubbled cheeks. But when I shave there is not the sound of a blade carving ancestral wood masks.

Afikpo is a double-descent culture. We are descended from both our matrilineal and patrilineal lines—Ikwunne and Ikwunna. It is a way of locating ourselves in an ever-changing world. So we claim descent in a double helix, like the DNA that forms us. We are from the lines that intersect, that liminal place of genetic encoding. My grand-father's people are Omaka Idume Chukwu, and my grandmother's people are Ajayi Mbeyi, Igbo on the first hand and Egu on the second.

The Egu were an aboriginal people, a root race that lived in the area of Afikpo from Neolithic times. A gentle people, it was said. Trusting, but strong when they needed to be, and fierce fighters. But they were also farmers and potters. Artists. They were a people with a complex cosmological relationship to the universe. A people whose elders, upon attaining enlightenment, wove a rope long enough to measure the day and the night. When they found the exact midpoint, the door to heaven, they threw the rope up and climbed it into the very heart of God, the rope dropping down, the clues of its weave the gift of the measure left for generations to come. Or so we've been told.

They were the first people, before others came. It was Egu, then Nkalu, then Ebri, and then Ohaodu. Then finally in the seventeenth century, Omaka Igbo Chukwu, using subterfuge and infiltration, conquered and assimilated the Egu.

No one knows anymore what the true meaning of the word Egu was, since the language of that culture was lost or subsumed in Igbo. But Igbo is a tonal language; pronounced certain ways, Egu means hunger, and with another inflection it can mean a desperate hunger, starvation almost. A hunger that can birth a world, drive us forward from the Stone Age, and then stutter into extinction and assimilation. Those who wouldn't join Omaka Igbo Chukwu were massacred—men, women, and children. A half-mile from the house I grew up in was a stretch of abandoned land that had been proclaimed an evil forest. Its name was ogbugbu umuruma—the slaughter of children. The last of my Egu ancestors was named Aja Mbeyi, and the first of my Afikpo ancestors was Omaka Chukwu.

By the time my great-grandmother was born, they were just a legend. Nobody told me about them until I was a teenager and I had a strange dream. I was fourteen. From the corner of my room a woman emerged in a green mist. She was very dark and wore white and her teeth were filed to points and she said in a hiss, "Wake up. Don't you know you are Egu?" It was so real that I searched for her when I woke. That was the first time I heard the word Egu. I asked my father and he said, "All that is in the past. We are not Egu. We are Ehugbo Omaka Ejeali." But Egu blood runs deep and the traits are still there. I wonder how much, though. They say about four percent of genes in people from Asia and Europe trace back to Neanderthals. What does it mean to walk and talk with the genes of a people that Homo sapiens exterminated, or as some claim, even ate into extinction? Neanderthals were so strong it is said their muscles bent their bones. All that strength and they were unable to save themselves. And what of Egu? Why couldn't they save themselves? It is true, though, what my father said; it's all in the past, but I can't help wondering if I am part of an unbroken chain of purpose stretching from 10,000 BCE to now. Is that what a people are?

My grandfather laughed when I told him my dream. He said God put human eyes on the front of our heads so we could see only into the hope of the future and not linger in a past we no longer understand. But he did say this: the oldest mask we wear in the Isiji manhood rites, abstract and carved from calabash shell, the only one of its kind, is from the Egu. Who we are, Omaka Chukwu or not, and how we become who we are, is a gift of Egu. That's why we call that mask mbubu: the first one, after the first people. Egu came up from the ground here, then Nkalu came, and Ebri and even Ohaodu. Long before Omaka Chukwu.

We are called Ehugbo Omaka Ejali because Omaka made a big sacrifice to own the land, but his atonement is that all his descendants wear the face of the dead. Ihu gu bu ihu mma, your face is the face of the spirits. That is what Egu are.

I touch my face. I feel for stubble. I find some. I shave again. Put down the razor. Splash water on my cheeks and look at my misted image in the bathroom mirror: ghostly.

THIS MAY NOT BE TRUE

1. I am a better man than my father ever was.
2. I have none of the anger for myself and the world that damaged him and his entire generation.
3. I have never cheated on a woman.
4. I have never slept with a married woman.
5. I haven't spent my life trying to make up to women for all the hurt my father caused my mother.
6. I am nothing like him.
7. I am exactly like him.
8. I do not have his temper.
9. I love that my face is his face.
10. I have forgiven myself for being a bad son, for being his son.

TRUCE

AND WHO DOESN'T yearn for their father to love them? And who doesn't decide how or when they should be loved and what the proof of it is? But in the end, who can control it? This yearning kills us all in the end.

But who can say what love is in the end? Is it my father saying the words I love you? Is it the ice cream he would buy us as a treat and forget in the car while he sat drinking in a bar? The same ice cream he would bring home, now a bowl of sugary milk? And wake us up to eat in the light of flickering storm lanterns? Even though it is full of red ants who have found it in the car and who drowned trying to feast? Even though we have to pull them out, rubbing their corpses into a red blur on napkins, careful not to ingest them? Is that the measure of love?

Or a hand striking your face, or a ring drawing blood when you were rude? A stunning blow to protect you from finding blows later in life that might kill you? A stunning blow that aggregates over time with other blows, physical and verbal, to make you reckless in the world? To seek out precisely the blows you were meant not to? Like that moment in a bar in Benin City where I got into an argument with a scarred-up gangster and smashed a bottle to menace him with. I remember the lazy smile as he leaned back and asked, "You break bottle for me?" I remember the languid way he drained his beer before breaking the bottle. I remember the small shrug and chuckle before he drew the jagged edge of his own bottle up his own arm, cutting a three-inch gash. "You see this?" he asked, pointing. "This is the least I will do to you."

I suppose that too is a kind of love.

CODA

BROTHER: I've got something for your book.

ME: Yes?

BROTHER: Yes, it's a joke about your face.

ME: Let's hear it.

BROTHER: How's your face feeling?

ME: Fine, why?

BROTHER: Cause it's killing me. Hahaha. [Pause.] It's good, right?

ME: It's a bit tired.

BROTHER: Fine, how about this one? Doctor, why are some jokes so painful?

ME: [Sigh.] Why?

BROTHER: It must be the punch lines.

ME: It's not about the face.

BROTHER: It will be when I punch you in the face, hahahaha.

ME: [Sigh.] I have to get back to work.

BROTHER: Fine, go be boring. [Pause.] Like your face.

COMFORT

IN LOS ANGELES, where I lived for thirteen years until recently, male grooming is as much part of the landscape of masculinity as the gym. If you wandered into any nail salon, littered among the graceful women would be a few men, like wildebeest among gazelles. Relaxing in massage chairs, flicking through old copies of *Elle* and *Cosmopolitan*, men get manicures and pedicures as casually as you may please. And these are not male models or wannabe actors, just regular men who work in mechanic shops, grocery checkouts, the DMV: men's men.

I was a regular at East West Nails (now defunct) that was right by my house. The beauticians were mostly Korean and older—middle-aged ladies. They chatted with each other as they worked, and many times to their clients. My favorite was a fifty-year-old who said, "Call me Margaret." When she knew I was a writer she would regale me with summaries of the romance novels she got from the library near her home in Koreatown. When I asked for the titles, she would say, "All in Korean, you can't understand." Then she would tell me about her husband, who couldn't hold his liquor and whom she loved to get drunk so she could watch him sing at karaoke. "Even drunk he have a good voice," she would say. "That's why I love him, you know? He's a good man with a good heart." Then she would tell me how bad I was at looking after my feet, but she forgave me because my toes were funny and small for a big man. "Small toe for big man is good, plant you deep in the ground. I tell my husband that I tell you everything. That you listen good and not make me feel bad." "Really," I said. "What did he say?" She laughed and said, "He get jealous. All man get jealous. But I tell him it's not like that. I tell him this man with small toe, he have a comfortable face. That's why I tell him everything."

Comfortable face. I liked it. Made me think of a well-worn armchair that I'd like to collapse into after a rough day. A face made for sitting in. Where one could sip a sweet spicy ginger tea and talk about love and books and karaoke. A face worn in by living, worn in by suffering, by pain, by loss, but also by laughter and joy and the gifts of love and friendship, of family, of travel, of generations of DNA blending to make a true mix of human. I think of all the stress and relief of razors scraping hair from my face. Of extreme weather. Of rain. Of sun. I think of all the people who have touched my face, slapped it, punched it, kissed it, washed it, shaved it. All of that human contact must leave some trace, some of the need and anger that motivated that touch. This face is softened by it all. Made supple by all the wonder it has beheld, all the kindness, all the generosity of life.

Comfortable face.

To be at peace with yourself. To sit in that place in West African thought that is calmness, serenity, sensitivity, insight, inspiration—a river, all flow yet relaxed. Or the stone at the bottom of the river—worn smooth and reflective by the flow around it, unchanging, undying, ota omi.

When asked what I would say about my face in this essay, I thought about what Margaret said, thought about my face as a worn-in leather armchair.

Come.

Sit here a while.

ABOUT THE AUTHOR

CHRIS ABANI is a novelist, poet, essayist, screen-writer, and playwright. Born in Nigeria to an Igbo father and English mother, he grew up in Afikpo, Nigeria, received a BA in English from Imo State University, Nigeria, an MA in English, Gender and Culture from Birkbeck College, University of London, and a PhD in Literature and Creative Writing from the University of Southern California. He has resided in the United States since 2001.

He is the recipient of the PEN USA Freedom-to-Write Award, the Prince Claus Award, a Lannan Literary Fellowship, a California Book Award, a Hurston/Wright Legacy Award, a PEN Beyond the Margins Award, the PEN Hemingway Book Prize, and a Guggenheim Award.

His fiction includes *The Secret History of Las Vegas*, *Song For Night*, *The Virgin of Flames*, *Becoming Abigail*, *GraceLand*, and *Masters of the Board*. His poetry collections are *Sanctificum*, *There Are No Names for Red*, *Feed Me The Sun – Collected Long Poems*, *Hands Washing Water*, *Dog Woman*, *Daphne's Lot*, and *Kalakuta Republic*. His work has been translated into French, Italian, Spanish, German, Swedish, Romanian, Hebrew, Macedonian, Ukrainian, Portuguese, Dutch, Bosnian, and Serbian.

Through his TED Talks, public speaking, and essays, Abani is known as an international voice on humanitarianism, art, ethics, and our shared political responsibility. His critical and personal essays have been featured in books on art and photography, as well as *Witness*, *Parkett*, *The New York Times*, *O Magazine*, and *BOMB*.

His many research interests include African poetics, world literature, 20th century anglophone literature, African presences in Medieval and

Renaissance culture, the living architecture of cities, West African music, postcolonial and transnational theory, robotics and consciousness, and Yoruba and Igbo philosophy and religion.

He is a Board of Trustees Professor of English at Northwestern University.

RESTLESS BOOKS is an independent publisher for readers and writers in search of new destinations, experiences, and perspectives. From Asia to the Americas, from Tehran to Tel Aviv, we deliver stories of discovery, adventure, dislocation, and transformation.

Our readers are passionate about other cultures and other languages. Restless is committed to bringing out the best of international literature—fiction, journalism, memoirs, poetry, travel writing, illustrated books, and more—that reflects the restlessness of our multiform lives.